SCRIPTURE
NOTEBOOK

Daniel

Read. Reflect. Respond.

DANIEL

Daniel's Captivity in Babylon

1 In the third year of the reign of King Jehoiakim of Judah, King Nebuchadnezzar of Babylon came to Jerusalem and laid siege to it. ² The Lord handed King Jehoiakim of Judah over to him, along with some of the vessels from the house of God. Nebuchadnezzar carried them to the land of Babylon, to the house of his god, and put the vessels in the treasury of his god.

³ The king ordered Ashpenaz, his chief eunuch, to bring some of the Israelites from the royal family and from the nobility — ⁴ young men without any physical defect, good-looking, suitable for instruction in all wisdom, knowledgeable, perceptive, and capable of serving in the king's palace. He was to teach them the Chaldean language and literature. ⁵ The king assigned them daily provisions from the royal food and from the wine that he drank. They were to be trained for three years, and at the end of that time they were to attend the king. ⁶ Among them, from the Judahites, were Daniel, Hananiah, Mishael, and Azariah. ⁷ The chief eunuch gave them names; he gave the name Belteshazzar to Daniel, Shadrach to Hananiah, Meshach to Mishael, and Abednego to Azariah.

Faithfulness in Babylon

⁸ Daniel determined that he would not defile himself with the king's food or with the wine he drank. So he asked permission from the chief eunuch not to defile himself. ⁹ God had granted Daniel kindness and compassion from the chief eunuch, ¹⁰ yet he said to Daniel, "I fear my lord the king, who assigned your food and drink. What if he sees your faces looking thinner than the other young men your age? You would endanger my life with the king."

¹¹ So Daniel said to the guard whom the chief eunuch had assigned to Daniel, Hananiah, Mishael, and Azariah, ¹² "Please test your servants for ten days. Let us be given vegetables to eat and water to drink. ¹³ Then examine our appearance and

the appearance of the young men who are eating the king's food, and deal with your servants based on what you see." [14] He agreed with them about this and tested them for ten days. [15] At the end of ten days they looked better and healthier than all the young men who were eating the king's food. [16] So the guard continued to remove their food and the wine they were to drink and gave them vegetables.

Faithfulness Rewarded

[17] God gave these four young men knowledge and understanding in every kind of literature and wisdom. Daniel also understood visions and dreams of every kind. [18] At the end of the time that the king had said to present them, the chief eunuch presented them to Nebuchadnezzar. [19] The king interviewed them, and among all of them, no one was found equal to Daniel, Hananiah, Mishael, and Azariah. So they began to attend the king. [20] In every matter of wisdom and understanding that the king consulted them about, he found them ten times better than all the magicians and mediums in his entire kingdom. [21] Daniel remained there until the first year of King Cyrus.

Nebuchadnezzar's Dream

2 In the second year of his reign, Nebuchadnezzar had dreams that troubled him, and sleep deserted him. [2] So the king gave orders to summon the magicians, mediums, sorcerers, and Chaldeans to tell the king his dreams. When they came and stood before the king, [3] he said to them, "I have had a dream and am anxious to understand it."

[4] The Chaldeans spoke to the king (Aramaic begins here): "May the king live forever. Tell your servants the dream, and we will give the interpretation."

[5] The king replied to the Chaldeans, "My word is final: If you don't tell me the dream and its interpretation, you will be torn

limb from limb, and your houses will be made a garbage dump. ⁶ But if you make the dream and its interpretation known to me, you'll receive gifts, a reward, and great honor from me. So make the dream and its interpretation known to me."

⁷ They answered a second time, "May the king tell the dream to his servants, and we will make known the interpretation."

⁸ The king replied, "I know for certain you are trying to gain some time, because you see that my word is final. ⁹ If you don't tell me the dream, there is one decree for you. You have conspired to tell me something false or fraudulent until the situation changes. So tell me the dream and I will know you can give me its interpretation."

¹⁰ The Chaldeans answered the king, "No one on earth can make known what the king requests. Consequently, no king, however great and powerful, has ever asked anything like this of any magician, medium, or Chaldean. ¹¹ What the king is asking is so difficult that no one can make it known to him except the gods, whose dwelling is not with mortals." ¹² Because of this, the king became violently angry and gave orders to destroy all the wise men of Babylon. ¹³ The decree was issued that the wise men were to be executed, and they searched for Daniel and his friends, to execute them.

¹⁴ Then Daniel responded with tact and discretion to Arioch, the captain of the king's guard, who had gone out to execute the wise men of Babylon. ¹⁵ He asked Arioch, the king's officer, "Why is the decree from the king so harsh?" Then Arioch explained the situation to Daniel. ¹⁶ So Daniel went and asked the king to give him some time, so that he could give the king the interpretation.

¹⁷ Then Daniel went to his house and told his friends Hananiah, Mishael, and Azariah about the matter, ¹⁸ urging them to ask the God of the heavens for mercy concerning this mystery, so Daniel and his friends would not be destroyed with the

rest of Babylon's wise men. ¹⁹ The mystery was then revealed to Daniel in a vision at night, and Daniel praised the God of the heavens ²⁰ and declared:

May the name of God
be praised forever and ever,
for wisdom and power belong to him.
²¹ He changes the times and seasons;
he removes kings and establishes kings.
He gives wisdom to the wise
and knowledge to those
who have understanding.
²² He reveals the deep and hidden things;
he knows what is in the darkness,
and light dwells with him.
²³ I offer thanks and praise to you,
God of my ancestors,
because you have given me
wisdom and power.
And now you have let me know
what we asked of you,
for you have let us know
the king's mystery.

²⁴ Therefore Daniel went to Arioch, whom the king had assigned to destroy the wise men of Babylon. He came and said to him, "Don't destroy the wise men of Babylon! Bring me before the king, and I will give him the interpretation." ²⁵ Then Arioch quickly brought Daniel before the king and said to him, "I have found a man among the Judean exiles who can let the king know the interpretation." ²⁶ The king said in reply to Daniel, whose name was Belteshazzar, "Are you able to tell me the dream I had and its interpretation?"

²⁷Daniel answered the king, "No wise man, medium, magician, or diviner is able to make known to the king the mystery he asked about. ²⁸But there is a God in heaven who reveals mysteries, and he has let King Nebuchadnezzar know what will happen in the last days. Your dream and the visions that came into your mind as you lay in bed were these: ²⁹Your Majesty, while you were in your bed, thoughts came to your mind about what will happen in the future. The revealer of mysteries has let you know what will happen. ³⁰As for me, this mystery has been revealed to me, not because I have more wisdom than anyone living, but in order that the interpretation might be made known to the king, and that you may understand the thoughts of your mind.

The Dream's Interpretation

³¹"Your Majesty, as you were watching, suddenly a colossal statue appeared. That statue, tall and dazzling, was standing in front of you, and its appearance was terrifying. ³²The head of the statue was pure gold, its chest and arms were silver, its stomach and thighs were bronze, ³³its legs were iron, and its feet were partly iron and partly fired clay. ³⁴As you were watching, a stone broke off without a hand touching it, struck the statue on its feet of iron and fired clay, and crushed them. ³⁵Then the iron, the fired clay, the bronze, the silver, and the gold were shattered and became like chaff from the summer threshing floors. The wind carried them away, and not a trace of them could be found. But the stone that struck the statue became a great mountain and filled the whole earth.

³⁶"This was the dream; now we will tell the king its interpretation. ³⁷Your Majesty, you are king of kings. The God of the heavens has given you sovereignty, power, strength, and glory. ³⁸Wherever people live — or wild animals, or birds of the sky — he has handed them over to you and made you ruler over them all. You are the head of gold.

39 "After you, there will arise another kingdom, inferior to yours, and then another, a third kingdom, of bronze, which will rule the whole earth. **40** A fourth kingdom will be as strong as iron; for iron crushes and shatters everything, and like iron that smashes, it will crush and smash all the others. **41** You saw the feet and toes, partly of a potter's fired clay and partly of iron — it will be a divided kingdom, though some of the strength of iron will be in it. You saw the iron mixed with clay, **42** and that the toes of the feet were partly iron and partly fired clay — part of the kingdom will be strong, and part will be brittle. **43** You saw the iron mixed with clay — the peoples will mix with one another but will not hold together, just as iron does not mix with fired clay.

44 "In the days of those kings, the God of the heavens will set up a kingdom that will never be destroyed, and this kingdom will not be left to another people. It will crush all these kingdoms and bring them to an end, but will itself endure forever. **45** You saw a stone break off from the mountain without a hand touching it, and it crushed the iron, bronze, fired clay, silver, and gold. The great God has told the king what will happen in the future. The dream is certain, and its interpretation reliable."

Nebuchadnezzar's Response

46 Then King Nebuchadnezzar fell facedown, worshiped Daniel, and gave orders to present an offering and incense to him. **47** The king said to Daniel, "Your God is indeed God of gods, Lord of kings, and a revealer of mysteries, since you were able to reveal this mystery." **48** Then the king promoted Daniel and gave him many generous gifts. He made him ruler over the entire province of Babylon and chief governor over all the wise men of Babylon. **49** At Daniel's request, the king appointed Shadrach, Meshach, and Abednego to manage the province of Babylon. But Daniel remained at the king's court.

Nebuchadnezzar's Gold Statue

3 King Nebuchadnezzar made a gold statue, ninety feet high and nine feet wide. He set it up on the plain of Dura in the province of Babylon. ² King Nebuchadnezzar sent word to assemble the satraps, prefects, governors, advisers, treasurers, judges, magistrates, and all the rulers of the provinces to attend the dedication of the statue King Nebuchadnezzar had set up. ³ So the satraps, prefects, governors, advisers, treasurers, judges, magistrates, and all the rulers of the provinces assembled for the dedication of the statue the king had set up. Then they stood before the statue Nebuchadnezzar had set up.

⁴ A herald loudly proclaimed, "People of every nation and language, you are commanded: ⁵ When you hear the sound of the horn, flute, zither, lyre, harp, drum, and every kind of music, you are to fall facedown and worship the gold statue that King Nebuchadnezzar has set up. ⁶ But whoever does not fall down and worship will immediately be thrown into a furnace of blazing fire."

⁷ Therefore, when all the people heard the sound of the horn, flute, zither, lyre, harp, and every kind of music, people of every nation and language fell down and worshiped the gold statue that King Nebuchadnezzar had set up.

The Furnace of Blazing Fire

⁸ Some Chaldeans took this occasion to come forward and maliciously accuse the Jews. ⁹ They said to King Nebuchadnezzar, "May the king live forever. ¹⁰ You as king have issued a decree that everyone who hears the sound of the horn, flute, zither, lyre, harp, drum, and every kind of music must fall down and worship the gold statue. ¹¹ Whoever does not fall down and worship will be thrown into a furnace of blazing fire. ¹² There are some Jews you have appointed to manage the province of

Babylon: Shadrach, Meshach, and Abednego. These men have ignored you, the king; they do not serve your gods or worship the gold statue you have set up."

¹³ Then in a furious rage Nebuchadnezzar gave orders to bring in Shadrach, Meshach, and Abednego. So these men were brought before the king. ¹⁴ Nebuchadnezzar asked them, "Shadrach, Meshach, and Abednego, is it true that you don't serve my gods or worship the gold statue I have set up? ¹⁵ Now if you're ready, when you hear the sound of the horn, flute, zither, lyre, harp, drum, and every kind of music, fall down and worship the statue I made. But if you don't worship it, you will immediately be thrown into a furnace of blazing fire — and who is the god who can rescue you from my power?"

¹⁶ Shadrach, Meshach, and Abednego replied to the king, "Nebuchadnezzar, we don't need to give you an answer to this question. ¹⁷ If the God we serve exists, then he can rescue us from the furnace of blazing fire, and he can rescue us from the power of you, the king. ¹⁸ But even if he does not rescue us, we want you as king to know that we will not serve your gods or worship the gold statue you set up."

¹⁹ Then Nebuchadnezzar was filled with rage, and the expression on his face changed toward Shadrach, Meshach, and Abednego. He gave orders to heat the furnace seven times more than was customary, ²⁰ and he commanded some of the best soldiers in his army to tie up Shadrach, Meshach, and Abednego and throw them into the furnace of blazing fire. ²¹ So these men, in their trousers, robes, head coverings, and other clothes, were tied up and thrown into the furnace of blazing fire. ²² Since the king's command was so urgent and the furnace extremely hot, the raging flames killed those men who carried up Shadrach, Meshach, and Abednego. ²³ And these three men, Shadrach, Meshach, and Abednego fell, bound, into the furnace of blazing fire.

Delivered from the Fire

24 Then King Nebuchadnezzar jumped up in alarm. He said to his advisers, "Didn't we throw three men, bound, into the fire?"

"Yes, of course, Your Majesty," they replied to the king.

25 He exclaimed, "Look! I see four men, not tied, walking around in the fire unharmed; and the fourth looks like a son of the gods."

26 Nebuchadnezzar then approached the door of the furnace of blazing fire and called, "Shadrach, Meshach, and Abednego, you servants of the Most High God — come out!" So Shadrach, Meshach, and Abednego came out of the fire. **27** When the satraps, prefects, governors, and the king's advisers gathered around, they saw that the fire had no effect on the bodies of these men: not a hair of their heads was singed, their robes were unaffected, and there was no smell of fire on them. **28** Nebuchadnezzar exclaimed, "Praise to the God of Shadrach, Meshach, and Abednego! He sent his angel and rescued his servants who trusted in him. They violated the king's command and risked their lives rather than serve or worship any god except their own God. **29** Therefore I issue a decree that anyone of any people, nation, or language who says anything offensive against the God of Shadrach, Meshach, and Abednego will be torn limb from limb and his house made a garbage dump. For there is no other god who is able to deliver like this." **30** Then the king rewarded Shadrach, Meshach, and Abednego in the province of Babylon.

Nebuchadnezzar's Proclamation

4 King Nebuchadnezzar,

To those of every people, nation, and language, who live on the whole earth:

May your prosperity increase. **2** I am pleased to tell you

about the miracles and wonders the Most High God has
done for me.

3   How great are his miracles,
     and how mighty his wonders!
     His kingdom is an eternal kingdom,
     and his dominion is from generation to generation.

The Dream

⁴ I, Nebuchadnezzar, was at ease in my house and flourishing in my
palace. ⁵ I had a dream, and it frightened me; while in my bed, the
images and visions in my mind alarmed me. ⁶ So I issued a decree
to bring all the wise men of Babylon to me in order that they might
make the dream's interpretation known to me. ⁷ When the magicians, mediums, Chaldeans, and diviners came in, I told them the
dream, but they could not make its interpretation known to me.

⁸ Finally Daniel, named Belteshazzar after the name of my
god — and a spirit of the holy gods is in him — came before
me. I told him the dream: ⁹ "Belteshazzar, head of the magicians, because I know that you have the spirit of the holy gods
and that no mystery puzzles you, explain to me the visions of
my dream that I saw, and its interpretation. ¹⁰ In the visions of
my mind as I was lying in bed, I saw this:
     There was a tree in the middle of the earth,
     and it was very tall.
11   The tree grew large and strong;
     its top reached to the sky,
     and it was visible to the ends of the earth.
12   Its leaves were beautiful, its fruit was abundant,
     and on it was food for all.
     Wild animals found shelter under it,
     the birds of the sky lived in its branches,
     and every creature was fed from it.

¹³ "As I was lying in my bed, I also saw in the visions of my mind a watcher, a holy one, coming down from heaven. ¹⁴ He called out loudly:

> Cut down the tree and chop off its branches;
> strip off its leaves and scatter its fruit.
> Let the animals flee from under it,
> and the birds from its branches.
>
> ¹⁵ But leave the stump with its roots in the ground
> and with a band of iron and bronze around it
> in the tender grass of the field.
> Let him be drenched with dew from the sky
> and share the plants of the earth
> with the animals.
>
> ¹⁶ Let his mind be changed from that of a human,
> and let him be given the mind of an animal
> for seven periods of time.
>
> ¹⁷ This word is by decree of the watchers,
> and the decision is by command
>   from the holy ones.
> This is so that the living will know
> that the Most High is ruler
> over human kingdoms.
> He gives them to anyone he wants
> and sets the lowliest of people over them.

¹⁸ This is the dream that I, King Nebuchadnezzar, had. Now, Belteshazzar, tell me the interpretation, because none of the wise men of my kingdom can make the interpretation known to me. But you can, because you have a spirit of the holy gods."

The Dream Interpreted

¹⁹ Then Daniel, whose name is Belteshazzar, was stunned for a moment, and his thoughts alarmed him. The king said, "Belteshazzar, don't let the dream or its interpretation alarm you."

Belteshazzar answered, "My lord, may the dream apply to those who hate you, and its interpretation to your enemies! 20 The tree you saw, which grew large and strong, whose top reached to the sky and was visible to the whole earth, 21 and whose leaves were beautiful and its fruit abundant — and on it was food for all, under it the wild animals lived, and in its branches the birds of the sky lived — 22 that tree is you, Your Majesty. For you have become great and strong: your greatness has grown and even reaches the sky, and your dominion extends to the ends of the earth.

23 "The king saw a watcher, a holy one, coming down from heaven and saying, 'Cut down the tree and destroy it, but leave the stump with its roots in the ground and with a band of iron and bronze around it in the tender grass of the field. Let him be drenched with dew from the sky and share food with the wild animals for seven periods of time.' 24 This is the interpretation, Your Majesty, and this is the decree of the Most High that has been issued against my lord the king: 25 You will be driven away from people to live with the wild animals. You will feed on grass like cattle and be drenched with dew from the sky for seven periods of time, until you acknowledge that the Most High is ruler over human kingdoms, and he gives them to anyone he wants. 26 As for the command to leave the tree's stump with its roots, your kingdom will be restored to you as soon as you acknowledge that Heaven rules. 27 Therefore, may my advice seem good to you my king. Separate yourself from your sins by doing what is right, and from your injustices by showing mercy to the needy. Perhaps there will be an extension of your prosperity."

The Sentence Executed

28 All this happened to King Nebuchadnezzar. 29 At the end of twelve months, as he was walking on the roof of the royal

palace in Babylon, ³⁰ the king exclaimed, "Is this not Babylon the Great that I have built to be a royal residence by my vast power and for my majestic glory?"

³¹ While the words were still in the king's mouth, a voice came from heaven: "King Nebuchadnezzar, to you it is declared that the kingdom has departed from you. ³² You will be driven away from people to live with the wild animals, and you will feed on grass like cattle for seven periods of time, until you acknowledge that the Most High is ruler over human kingdoms, and he gives them to anyone he wants."

³³ At that moment the message against Nebuchadnezzar was fulfilled. He was driven away from people. He ate grass like cattle, and his body was drenched with dew from the sky, until his hair grew like eagles' feathers and his nails like birds' claws.

Nebuchadnezzar's Praise

³⁴ But at the end of those days, I, Nebuchadnezzar, looked up to heaven, and my sanity returned to me. Then I praised the Most High and honored and glorified him who lives forever:

For his dominion is an everlasting dominion,
and his kingdom is from generation to generation.
³⁵ All the inhabitants of the earth are counted as nothing,
and he does what he wants with the army of heaven
and the inhabitants of the earth.
There is no one who can block his hand
or say to him, "What have you done?"

³⁶ At that time my sanity returned to me, and my majesty and splendor returned to me for the glory of my kingdom. My advisers and my nobles sought me out, I was reestablished over my kingdom, and even more greatness came to me. ³⁷ Now I, Nebuchadnezzar, praise, exalt, and glorify the King of the heavens, because all his works are true and his ways are just. He is able to humble those who walk in pride.

Belshazzar's Feast

5 King Belshazzar held a great feast for a thousand of his nobles and drank wine in their presence. ² Under the influence of the wine, Belshazzar gave orders to bring in the gold and silver vessels that his predecessor Nebuchadnezzar had taken from the temple in Jerusalem, so that the king and his nobles, wives, and concubines could drink from them. ³ So they brought in the gold vessels that had been taken from the temple, the house of God in Jerusalem, and the king and his nobles, wives, and concubines drank from them. ⁴ They drank the wine and praised their gods made of gold and silver, bronze, iron, wood, and stone.

The Handwriting on the Wall

⁵ At that moment the fingers of a man's hand appeared and began writing on the plaster of the king's palace wall next to the lampstand. As the king watched the hand that was writing, ⁶ his face turned pale, and his thoughts so terrified him that he soiled himself and his knees knocked together. ⁷ The king shouted to bring in the mediums, Chaldeans, and diviners. He said to these wise men of Babylon, "Whoever reads this inscription and gives me its interpretation will be clothed in purple, have a gold chain around his neck, and have the third highest position in the kingdom." ⁸ So all the king's wise men came in, but none could read the inscription or make its interpretation known to him. ⁹ Then King Belshazzar became even more terrified, his face turned pale, and his nobles were bewildered.

¹⁰ Because of the outcry of the king and his nobles, the queen came to the banquet hall. "May the king live forever," she said. "Don't let your thoughts terrify you or your face be pale. ¹¹ There is a man in your kingdom who has a spirit of the holy gods in him. In the days of your predecessor he was found to

have insight, intelligence, and wisdom like the wisdom of the gods. Your predecessor, King Nebuchadnezzar, appointed him chief of the magicians, mediums, Chaldeans, and diviners. Your own predecessor, the king, **¹²** did this because Daniel, the one the king named Belteshazzar, was found to have an extraordinary spirit, knowledge and intelligence, and the ability to interpret dreams, explain riddles, and solve problems. Therefore, summon Daniel, and he will give the interpretation."

Daniel before the King

¹³ Then Daniel was brought before the king. The king said to him, "Are you Daniel, one of the Judean exiles that my predecessor the king brought from Judah? **¹⁴** I've heard that you have a spirit of the gods in you, and that insight, intelligence, and extraordinary wisdom are found in you. **¹⁵** Now the wise men and mediums were brought before me to read this inscription and make its interpretation known to me, but they could not give its interpretation. **¹⁶** However, I have heard about you that you can give interpretations and solve problems. Therefore, if you can read this inscription and give me its interpretation, you will be clothed in purple, have a gold chain around your neck, and have the third highest position in the kingdom."

¹⁷ Then Daniel answered the king, "You may keep your gifts and give your rewards to someone else; however, I will read the inscription for the king and make the interpretation known to him. **¹⁸** Your Majesty, the Most High God gave sovereignty, greatness, glory, and majesty to your predecessor Nebuchadnezzar. **¹⁹** Because of the greatness he gave him, all peoples, nations, and languages were terrified and fearful of him. He killed anyone he wanted and kept alive anyone he wanted; he exalted anyone he wanted and humbled anyone he wanted. **²⁰** But when his heart was exalted and his spirit became arrogant, he was deposed from his royal throne and his glory was

taken from him. ²¹ He was driven away from people, his mind was like an animal's, he lived with the wild donkeys, he was fed grass like cattle, and his body was drenched with dew from the sky until he acknowledged that the Most High God is ruler over human kingdoms and sets anyone he wants over them.

²² "But you his successor, Belshazzar, have not humbled your heart, even though you knew all this. ²³ Instead, you have exalted yourself against the Lord of the heavens. The vessels from his house were brought to you, and as you and your nobles, wives, and concubines drank wine from them, you praised the gods made of silver and gold, bronze, iron, wood, and stone, which do not see or hear or understand. But you have not glorified the God who holds your life-breath in his hand and who controls the whole course of your life. ²⁴ Therefore, he sent the hand, and this writing was inscribed.

The Inscription's Interpretation

²⁵ "This is the writing that was inscribed: MENE, MENE, TEKEL, and PARSIN. ²⁶ This is the interpretation of the message:
'Mene' means that God has numbered the days of your kingdom and brought it to an end.
²⁷ 'Tekel' means that you have been weighed on the balance and found deficient.
²⁸ 'Peres' means that your kingdom has been divided and given to the Medes and Persians."

²⁹ Then Belshazzar gave an order, and they clothed Daniel in purple, placed a gold chain around his neck, and issued a proclamation concerning him that he should be the third ruler in the kingdom.

³⁰ That very night Belshazzar the king of the Chaldeans was killed, ³¹ and Darius the Mede received the kingdom at the age of sixty-two.

The Plot against Daniel

6 Darius decided to appoint 120 satraps over the kingdom, stationed throughout the realm, ² and over them three administrators, including Daniel. These satraps would be accountable to them so that the king would not be defrauded. ³ Daniel distinguished himself above the administrators and satraps because he had an extraordinary spirit, so the king planned to set him over the whole realm. ⁴ The administrators and satraps, therefore, kept trying to find a charge against Daniel regarding the kingdom. But they could find no charge or corruption, for he was trustworthy, and no negligence or corruption was found in him. ⁵ Then these men said, "We will never find any charge against this Daniel unless we find something against him concerning the law of his God."

⁶ So the administrators and satraps went together to the king and said to him, "May King Darius live forever. ⁷ All the administrators of the kingdom — the prefects, satraps, advisers, and governors — have agreed that the king should establish an ordinance and enforce an edict that, for thirty days, anyone who petitions any god or man except you, the king, will be thrown into the lions' den. ⁸ Therefore, Your Majesty, establish the edict and sign the document so that, as a law of the Medes and Persians, it is irrevocable and cannot be changed." ⁹ So King Darius signed the written edict.

Daniel in the Lions' Den

¹⁰ When Daniel learned that the document had been signed, he went into his house. The windows in its upstairs room opened toward Jerusalem, and three times a day he got down on his knees, prayed, and gave thanks to his God, just as he had done before. ¹¹ Then these men went as a group and found Daniel petitioning and imploring his God. ¹² So they approached the king and asked about his edict: "Didn't you sign an edict that for

thirty days any person who petitions any god or man except you, the king, will be thrown into the lions' den?"

The king answered, "As a law of the Medes and Persians, the order stands and is irrevocable."

¹³ Then they replied to the king, "Daniel, one of the Judean exiles, has ignored you, the king, and the edict you signed, for he prays three times a day." ¹⁴ As soon as the king heard this, he was very displeased; he set his mind on rescuing Daniel and made every effort until sundown to deliver him.

¹⁵ Then these men went together to the king and said to him, "You know, Your Majesty, that it is a law of the Medes and Persians that no edict or ordinance the king establishes can be changed."

¹⁶ So the king gave the order, and they brought Daniel and threw him into the lions' den. The king said to Daniel, "May your God, whom you continually serve, rescue you!" ¹⁷ A stone was brought and placed over the mouth of the den. The king sealed it with his own signet ring and with the signet rings of his nobles, so that nothing in regard to Daniel could be changed. ¹⁸ Then the king went to his palace and spent the night fasting. No diversions were brought to him, and he could not sleep.

Daniel Released

¹⁹ At the first light of dawn the king got up and hurried to the lions' den. ²⁰ When he reached the den, he cried out in anguish to Daniel. "Daniel, servant of the living God," the king said, "has your God, whom you continually serve, been able to rescue you from the lions?"

²¹ Then Daniel spoke with the king: "May the king live forever. ²² My God sent his angel and shut the lions' mouths; and they haven't harmed me, for I was found innocent before him. And also before you, Your Majesty, I have not done harm."

²³ The king was overjoyed and gave orders to take Daniel out of the den. When Daniel was brought up from the den, he was

found to be unharmed, for he trusted in his God. ²⁴ The king then gave the command, and those men who had maliciously accused Daniel were brought and thrown into the lions' den — they, their children, and their wives. They had not reached the bottom of the den before the lions overpowered them and crushed all their bones.

Darius Honors God

²⁵ Then King Darius wrote to those of every people, nation, and language who live on the whole earth: "May your prosperity abound. ²⁶ I issue a decree that in all my royal dominion, people must tremble in fear before the God of Daniel:

> For he is the living God,
> and he endures forever;
> his kingdom will never be destroyed,
> and his dominion has no end.
> ²⁷ He rescues and delivers;
> he performs signs and wonders
> in the heavens and on the earth,
> for he has rescued Daniel
> from the power of the lions."

²⁸ So Daniel prospered during the reign of Darius and the reign of Cyrus the Persian.

Daniel's Vision of the Four Beasts

7 In the first year of King Belshazzar of Babylon, Daniel had a dream with visions in his mind as he was lying in his bed. He wrote down the dream, and here is the summary of his account. ² Daniel said, "In my vision at night I was watching, and suddenly the four winds of heaven stirred up the great sea. ³ Four huge beasts came up from the sea, each different from the other.

4 "The first was like a lion but had eagle's wings. I continued watching until its wings were torn off. It was lifted up from the ground, set on its feet like a man, and given a human mind.

5 "Suddenly, another beast appeared, a second one, that looked like a bear. It was raised up on one side, with three ribs in its mouth between its teeth. It was told, 'Get up! Gorge yourself on flesh.'

6 "After this, while I was watching, suddenly another beast appeared. It was like a leopard with four wings of a bird on its back. It had four heads, and it was given dominion.

7 "After this, while I was watching in the night visions, suddenly a fourth beast appeared, frightening and dreadful, and incredibly strong, with large iron teeth. It devoured and crushed, and it trampled with its feet whatever was left. It was different from all the beasts before it, and it had ten horns.

8 "While I was considering the horns, suddenly another horn, a little one, came up among them, and three of the first horns were uprooted before it. And suddenly in this horn there were eyes like the eyes of a human and a mouth that was speaking arrogantly.

The Ancient of Days and the Son of Man

9 "As I kept watching,

> thrones were set in place,
> and the Ancient of Days took his seat.
> His clothing was white like snow,
> and the hair of his head like whitest wool.
> His throne was flaming fire;
> its wheels were blazing fire.

10   A river of fire was flowing,
> coming out from his presence.
> Thousands upon thousands served him;
> ten thousand times ten thousand stood before him.

The court was convened,
and the books were opened.

¹¹ "I watched, then, because of the sound of the arrogant words the horn was speaking. As I continued watching, the beast was killed and its body destroyed and given over to the burning fire. ¹² As for the rest of the beasts, their dominion was removed, but an extension of life was granted to them for a certain period of time. ¹³ I continued watching in the night visions,
and suddenly one like a son of man
was coming with the clouds of heaven.
He approached the Ancient of Days
and was escorted before him.
¹⁴ He was given dominion
and glory and a kingdom,
so that those of every people,
nation, and language
should serve him.
His dominion is an everlasting dominion
that will not pass away,
and his kingdom is one
that will not be destroyed.

Interpretation of the Vision

¹⁵ "As for me, Daniel, my spirit was deeply distressed within me, and the visions in my mind terrified me. ¹⁶ I approached one of those who were standing by and asked him to clarify all this. So he let me know the interpretation of these things: ¹⁷ 'These huge beasts, four in number, are four kings who will rise from the earth. ¹⁸ But the holy ones of the Most High will receive the kingdom and possess it forever, yes, forever and ever.'

¹⁹ "Then I wanted to be clear about the fourth beast, the one different from all the others, extremely terrifying, with iron

teeth and bronze claws, devouring, crushing, and trampling with its feet whatever was left. ²⁰ I also wanted to know about the ten horns on its head and about the other horn that came up, before which three fell — the horn that had eyes, and a mouth that spoke arrogantly, and that looked bigger than the others. ²¹ As I was watching, this horn waged war against the holy ones and was prevailing over them ²² until the Ancient of Days arrived and a judgment was given in favor of the holy ones of the Most High, for the time had come, and the holy ones took possession of the kingdom.

²³ "This is what he said: 'The fourth beast will be a fourth kingdom on the earth, different from all the other kingdoms. It will devour the whole earth, trample it down, and crush it. ²⁴ The ten horns are ten kings who will rise from this kingdom. Another king, different from the previous ones, will rise after them and subdue three kings. ²⁵ He will speak words against the Most High and oppress the holy ones of the Most High. He will intend to change religious festivals and laws, and the holy ones will be handed over to him for a time, times, and half a time. ²⁶ But the court will convene, and his dominion will be taken away, to be completely destroyed forever. ²⁷ The kingdom, dominion, and greatness of the kingdoms under all of heaven will be given to the people, the holy ones of the Most High. His kingdom will be an everlasting kingdom, and all rulers will serve and obey him.'

²⁸ "This is the end of the account. As for me, Daniel, my thoughts terrified me greatly, and my face turned pale, but I kept the matter to myself."

The Vision of a Ram and a Goat

8 In the third year of King Belshazzar's reign, a vision appeared to me, Daniel, after the one that had appeared to me earlier. ² I saw the vision, and as I watched, I was in the fortress city of

Susa, in the province of Elam. I saw in the vision that I was beside the Ulai Canal. ³ I looked up, and there was a ram standing beside the canal. He had two horns. The two horns were long, but one was longer than the other, and the longer one came up last. ⁴ I saw the ram charging to the west, the north, and the south. No animal could stand against him, and there was no rescue from his power. He did whatever he wanted and became great.

⁵ As I was observing, a male goat appeared, coming from the west across the surface of the entire earth without touching the ground. The goat had a conspicuous horn between his eyes. ⁶ He came toward the two-horned ram I had seen standing beside the canal and rushed at him with savage fury. ⁷ I saw him approaching the ram, and infuriated with him, he struck the ram, breaking his two horns, and the ram was not strong enough to stand against him. The goat threw him to the ground and trampled him, and there was no one to rescue the ram from his power. ⁸ Then the male goat acted even more arrogantly, but when he became powerful, the large horn was broken. Four conspicuous horns came up in its place, pointing toward the four winds of heaven.

The Little Horn

⁹ From one of them a little horn emerged and grew extensively toward the south and the east and toward the beautiful land. ¹⁰ It grew as high as the heavenly army, made some of the army and some of the stars fall to the earth, and trampled them. ¹¹ It acted arrogantly even against the Prince of the heavenly army; it revoked his regular sacrifice and overthrew the place of his sanctuary. ¹² In the rebellion, the army was given up, together with the regular sacrifice. The horn threw truth to the ground and was successful in what it did.

¹³ Then I heard a holy one speaking, and another holy one said to the speaker, "How long will the events of this vision last — the

regular sacrifice, the rebellion that makes desolate, and the giving over of the sanctuary and of the army to be trampled?"

¹⁴ He said to me, "For 2,300 evenings and mornings; then the sanctuary will be restored."

Interpretation of the Vision

¹⁵ While I, Daniel, was watching the vision and trying to understand it, there stood before me someone who appeared to be a man. ¹⁶ I heard a human voice calling from the middle of the Ulai: "Gabriel, explain the vision to this man."

¹⁷ So he approached where I was standing; when he came near, I was terrified and fell facedown. "Son of man," he said to me, "understand that the vision refers to the time of the end." ¹⁸ While he was speaking to me, I fell into a deep sleep, with my face to the ground. Then he touched me, made me stand up, ¹⁹ and said, "I am here to tell you what will happen at the conclusion of the time of wrath, because it refers to the appointed time of the end. ²⁰ The two-horned ram that you saw represents the kings of Media and Persia. ²¹ The shaggy goat represents the king of Greece, and the large horn between his eyes represents the first king. ²² The four horns that took the place of the broken horn represent four kingdoms. They will rise from that nation, but without its power.

²³ Near the end of their kingdoms,
when the rebels have reached
the full measure of their sin,
a ruthless king, skilled in intrigue,
will come to the throne.
²⁴ His power will be great,
but it will not be his own.
He will cause outrageous destruction
and succeed in whatever he does.

> He will destroy the powerful
> along with the holy people.
> 25 He will cause deceit to prosper
> through his cunning and by his influence,
> and in his own mind he will exalt himself.
> He will destroy many in a time of peace;
> he will even stand against the Prince of princes.
> Yet he will be broken — not by human hands.
> 26 The vision of the evenings and the mornings
> that has been told is true.
> Now you are to seal up the vision
> because it refers to many days in the future."

27 I, Daniel, was overcome and lay sick for days. Then I got up and went about the king's business. I was greatly disturbed by the vision and could not understand it.

Daniel's Prayer

9 In the first year of Darius, the son of Ahasuerus, a Mede by birth, who was made king over the Chaldean kingdom — 2 in the first year of his reign, I, Daniel, understood from the books according to the word of the LORD to the prophet Jeremiah that the number of years for the desolation of Jerusalem would be seventy. 3 So I turned my attention to the Lord God to seek him by prayer and petitions, with fasting, sackcloth, and ashes.

4 I prayed to the LORD my God and confessed:

Ah, Lord — the great and awe-inspiring God who keeps his gracious covenant with those who love him and keep his commands — 5 we have sinned, done wrong, acted wickedly, rebelled, and turned away from your commands and ordinances. 6 We have not listened to your servants the prophets, who spoke in your name to our kings, leaders, ancestors, and all the people of the land.

[7] Lord, righteousness belongs to you, but this day public shame belongs to us: the men of Judah, the residents of Jerusalem, and all Israel — those who are near and those who are far, in all the countries where you have banished them because of the disloyalty they have shown toward you. [8] LORD, public shame belongs to us, our kings, our leaders, and our ancestors, because we have sinned against you. [9] Compassion and forgiveness belong to the Lord our God, though we have rebelled against him [10] and have not obeyed the LORD our God by following his instructions that he set before us through his servants the prophets.

[11] All Israel has broken your law and turned away, refusing to obey you. The promised curse written in the law of Moses, the servant of God, has been poured out on us because we have sinned against him. [12] He has carried out his words that he spoke against us and against our rulers by bringing on us a disaster that is so great that nothing like what has been done to Jerusalem has ever been done under all of heaven. [13] Just as it is written in the law of Moses, all this disaster has come on us, yet we have not sought the favor of the LORD our God by turning from our iniquities and paying attention to your truth. [14] So the LORD kept the disaster in mind and brought it on us, for the LORD our God is righteous in all he has done. But we have not obeyed him.

[15] Now, Lord our God — who brought your people out of the land of Egypt with a strong hand and made your name renowned as it is this day — we have sinned, we have acted wickedly. [16] Lord, in keeping with all your righteous acts, may your anger and wrath turn away from your city Jerusalem, your holy mountain; for because of our sins and the iniquities of our ancestors, Jerusalem and

your people have become an object of ridicule to all those around us.

¹⁷ Therefore, our God, hear the prayer and the petitions of your servant. Make your face shine on your desolate sanctuary for the Lord's sake. ¹⁸ Listen closely, my God, and hear. Open your eyes and see our desolations and the city that bears your name. For we are not presenting our petitions before you based on our righteous acts, but based on your abundant compassion. ¹⁹ Lord, hear! Lord, forgive! Lord, listen and act! My God, for your own sake, do not delay, because your city and your people bear your name.

The Seventy Weeks of Years

²⁰ While I was speaking, praying, confessing my sin and the sin of my people Israel, and presenting my petition before the Lord my God concerning the holy mountain of my God— ²¹ while I was praying, Gabriel, the man I had seen in the first vision, reached me in my extreme weariness, about the time of the evening offering. ²² He gave me this explanation: "Daniel, I've come now to give you understanding. ²³ At the beginning of your petitions an answer went out, and I have come to give it, for you are treasured by God. So consider the message and understand the vision:

24   Seventy weeks are decreed
      about your people and your holy city —
      to bring the rebellion to an end,
      to put a stop to sin,
      to atone for iniquity,
      to bring in everlasting righteousness,
      to seal up vision and prophecy,
      and to anoint the most holy place.
25   Know and understand this:

From the issuing of the decree
to restore and rebuild Jerusalem
until an Anointed One, the ruler,
will be seven weeks and sixty-two weeks.
It will be rebuilt with a plaza and a moat,
but in difficult times.

26 After those sixty-two weeks
the Anointed One will be cut off
and will have nothing.
The people of the coming ruler
will destroy the city and the sanctuary.
The end will come with a flood,
and until the end there will be war;
desolations are decreed.

27 He will make a firm covenant
with many for one week,
but in the middle of the week
he will put a stop to sacrifice and offering.
And the abomination of desolation
will be on a wing of the temple
until the decreed destruction
is poured out on the desolator."

Vision of a Glorious One

10 In the third year of King Cyrus of Persia, a message was revealed to Daniel, who was named Belteshazzar. The message was true and was about a great conflict. He understood the message and had understanding of the vision.

² In those days I, Daniel, was mourning for three full weeks. ³ I didn't eat any rich food, no meat or wine entered my mouth, and I didn't put any oil on my body until the three weeks were over. ⁴ On the twenty-fourth day of the first month, as I was standing on the bank of the great river, the Tigris, ⁵ I looked up,

and there was a man dressed in linen, with a belt of gold from Uphaz around his waist. ⁶ His body was like beryl, his face like the brilliance of lightning, his eyes like flaming torches, his arms and feet like the gleam of polished bronze, and the sound of his words like the sound of a multitude.

⁷ Only I, Daniel, saw the vision. The men who were with me did not see it, but a great terror fell on them, and they ran and hid. ⁸ I was left alone, looking at this great vision. No strength was left in me; my face grew deathly pale, and I was powerless. ⁹ I heard the words he said, and when I heard them I fell into a deep sleep, with my face to the ground.

Angelic Conflict

¹⁰ Suddenly, a hand touched me and set me shaking on my hands and knees. ¹¹ He said to me, "Daniel, you are a man treasured by God. Understand the words that I'm saying to you. Stand on your feet, for I have now been sent to you." After he said this to me, I stood trembling.

¹² "Don't be afraid, Daniel," he said to me, "for from the first day that you purposed to understand and to humble yourself before your God, your prayers were heard. I have come because of your prayers. ¹³ But the prince of the kingdom of Persia opposed me for twenty-one days. Then Michael, one of the chief princes, came to help me after I had been left there with the kings of Persia. ¹⁴ Now I have come to help you understand what will happen to your people in the last days, for the vision refers to those days."

¹⁵ While he was saying these words to me, I turned my face toward the ground and was speechless. ¹⁶ Suddenly one with human likeness touched my lips. I opened my mouth and said to the one standing in front of me, "My lord, because of the vision, anguish overwhelms me and I am powerless. ¹⁷ How can someone like me, your servant, speak with someone like

you, my lord? Now I have no strength, and there is no breath in me."

18 Then the one with a human appearance touched me again and strengthened me. 19 He said, "Don't be afraid, you who are treasured by God. Peace to you; be very strong!"

As he spoke to me, I was strengthened and said, "Let my lord speak, for you have strengthened me."

20 He said, "Do you know why I've come to you? I must return at once to fight against the prince of Persia, and when I leave, the prince of Greece will come. 21 However, I will tell you what is recorded in the book of truth. (No one has the courage to support me against those princes except Michael, your prince. 1 In the first year of Darius the Mede, I stood up to strengthen and protect him.) 2 Now I will tell you the truth.

Prophecies about Persia and Greece

"Three more kings will arise in Persia, and the fourth will be far richer than the others. By the power he gains through his riches, he will stir up everyone against the kingdom of Greece. 3 Then a warrior king will arise; he will rule a vast realm and do whatever he wants. 4 But as soon as he is established, his kingdom will be broken up and divided to the four winds of heaven, but not to his descendants; it will not be the same kingdom that he ruled, because his kingdom will be uprooted and will go to others besides them.

Kings of the South and the North

5 "The king of the South will grow powerful, but one of his commanders will grow more powerful and will rule a kingdom greater than his. 6 After some years they will form an alliance, and the daughter of the king of the South will go to the king of the North to seal the agreement. She will not retain power, and his strength will not endure. She will be given up, together

with her entourage, her father, and the one who supported her during those times. ⁷In the place of the king of the South, one from her family will rise up, come against the army, and enter the fortress of the king of the North. He will take action against them and triumph. ⁸He will take even their gods captive to Egypt, with their metal images and their precious articles of silver and gold. For some years he will stay away from the king of the North, ⁹who will enter the kingdom of the king of the South and then return to his own land.

¹⁰"His sons will mobilize for war and assemble a large number of armed forces. They will advance, sweeping through like a flood, and will again wage war as far as his fortress. ¹¹Infuriated, the king of the South will march out to fight with the king of the North, who will raise a large army, but they will be handed over to his enemy. ¹²When the army is carried off, he will become arrogant and cause tens of thousands to fall, but he will not triumph. ¹³The king of the North will again raise a multitude larger than the first. After some years he will advance with a great army and many supplies.

¹⁴"In those times many will rise up against the king of the South. Violent ones among your own people will assert themselves to fulfill a vision, but they will fail. ¹⁵Then the king of the North will come, build up a siege ramp, and capture a well-fortified city. The forces of the South will not stand; even their select troops will not be able to resist. ¹⁶The king of the North who comes against him will do whatever he wants, and no one can oppose him. He will establish himself in the beautiful land with total destruction in his hand. ¹⁷He will resolve to come with the force of his whole kingdom and will reach an agreement with him. He will give him a daughter in marriage to destroy it, but she will not stand with him or support him. ¹⁸Then he will turn his attention to the coasts and islands and capture many. But a commander will put an end to his taunting; instead, he will

turn his taunts against him. ¹⁹ He will turn his attention back to the fortresses of his own land, but he will stumble, fall, and be no more.

²⁰ "In his place one will arise who will send out a tax collector for the glory of the kingdom; but within a few days he will be broken, though not in anger or in battle.

²¹ "In his place a despised person will arise; royal honors will not be given to him, but he will come during a time of peace and seize the kingdom by intrigue. ²² A flood of forces will be swept away before him; they will be broken, as well as the covenant prince. ²³ After an alliance is made with him, he will act deceitfully. He will rise to power with a small nation. ²⁴ During a time of peace, he will come into the richest parts of the province and do what his fathers and predecessors never did. He will lavish plunder, loot, and wealth on his followers, and he will make plans against fortified cities, but only for a time.

²⁵ "With a large army he will stir up his power and his courage against the king of the South. The king of the South will prepare for battle with an extremely large and powerful army, but he will not succeed, because plots will be made against him. ²⁶ Those who eat his provisions will destroy him; his army will be swept away, and many will fall slain. ²⁷ The two kings, whose hearts are bent on evil, will speak lies at the same table but to no avail, for still the end will come at the appointed time. ²⁸ The king of the North will return to his land with great wealth, but his heart will be set against the holy covenant; he will take action, then return to his own land.

²⁹ "At the appointed time he will come again to the South, but this time will not be like the first. ³⁰ Ships of Kittim will come against him, and being intimidated, he will withdraw. Then he will rage against the holy covenant and take action. On his return, he will favor those who abandon the holy covenant. ³¹ His forces will rise up and desecrate the temple fortress. They will

abolish the regular sacrifice and set up the abomination of desolation. ³² With flattery he will corrupt those who act wickedly toward the covenant, but the people who know their God will be strong and take action. ³³ Those who have insight among the people will give understanding to many, yet they will fall by the sword and flame, and they will be captured and plundered for a time. ³⁴ When they fall, they will be helped by some, but many others will join them insincerely. ³⁵ Some of those who have insight will fall so that they may be refined, purified, and cleansed until the time of the end, for it will still come at the appointed time.

³⁶ "Then the king will do whatever he wants. He will exalt and magnify himself above every god, and he will say outrageous things against the God of gods. He will be successful until the time of wrath is completed, because what has been decreed will be accomplished. ³⁷ He will not show regard for the gods of his ancestors, the god desired by women, or for any other god, because he will magnify himself above all. ³⁸ Instead, he will honor a god of fortresses — a god his ancestors did not know — with gold, silver, precious stones, and riches. ³⁹ He will deal with the strongest fortresses with the help of a foreign god. He will greatly honor those who acknowledge him, making them rulers over many and distributing land as a reward.

⁴⁰ "At the time of the end, the king of the South will engage him in battle, but the king of the North will storm against him with chariots, horsemen, and many ships. He will invade countries and sweep through them like a flood. ⁴¹ He will also invade the beautiful land, and many will fall. But these will escape from his power: Edom, Moab, and the prominent people of the Ammonites. ⁴² He will extend his power against the countries, and not even the land of Egypt will escape. ⁴³ He will get control over the hidden treasures of gold and silver and over all the riches of Egypt. The Libyans and Cushites will also be

in submission. **44** But reports from the east and the north will terrify him, and he will go out with great fury to annihilate and completely destroy many. **45** He will pitch his royal tents between the sea and the beautiful holy mountain, but he will meet his end with no one to help him.

12

At that time
Michael, the great prince
who stands watch over your people, will rise up.
There will be a time of distress
such as never has occurred
since nations came into being until that time.
But at that time all your people
who are found written in the book
   will escape.

2 Many who sleep in the dust
of the earth will awake,
some to eternal life,
and some to disgrace and eternal contempt.

3 Those who have insight will shine
like the bright expanse of the heavens,
and those who lead many to righteousness,
like the stars forever and ever.

4 "But you, Daniel, keep these words secret and seal the book until the time of the end. Many will roam about, and knowledge will increase."

5 Then I, Daniel, looked, and two others were standing there, one on this bank of the river and one on the other. **6** One of them said to the man dressed in linen, who was above the water of the river, "How long until the end of these wondrous things?" **7** Then I heard the man dressed in linen, who was above the water of the river. He raised both his hands toward heaven and swore by him who lives eternally that it would be for a time,

times, and half a time. When the power of the holy people is shattered, all these things will be completed.

⁸ I heard but did not understand. So I asked, "My lord, what will be the outcome of these things?"

⁹ He said, "Go on your way, Daniel, for the words are secret and sealed until the time of the end. ¹⁰ Many will be purified, cleansed, and refined, but the wicked will act wickedly; none of the wicked will understand, but those who have insight will understand. ¹¹ From the time the daily sacrifice is abolished and the abomination of desolation is set up, there will be 1,290 days. ¹² Happy is the one who waits for and reaches 1,335 days. ¹³ But as for you, go on your way to the end; you will rest, and then you will rise to receive your allotted inheritance at the end of the days."